Briefings

Briefings

Poems Small and Easy

•••

A. R. AMMONS

W · W · NORTON & COMPANY · INC ·

NEW YORK

for John Logan

Contents

Acknowledgments

I thank the editors of the following periodicals for first publishing the poems listed:

Poetry: "Cougar," "This Bright Day," "September Drift," "Working Still," "Dominion," "Treaties," "Project," "Play," "Countering," "Square," "Reversal," "Admission," "Mission," "Cut the Grass," "Pluralist," "Here & Now."

The Hudson Review: "After Yesterday," "Father," "Poetics," "Making," "Round," "Gain," "Concerning the Exclusions of the Object."

The New York Times: "Center," "Mechanics," "Saying," "Crevice."

The Quest: "He Held Radical Light," "The Woodsroad," "WCW," "Elegy for a Jet Pilot."

Epos: "Event," "This Black Rich Country," "Look for My White Self."

Lillabulero: "Tight," "Autumn Song," "Medium."

Southern Poetry Review: "Wagons," "Working with Tools," "The Run-Through."

Abraxas: "The Quince Bush," "The Confirmers."

Accent: "Sumerian," "Hymn IV."

Choice: "Spinejacking."

Modern Occasions: "The City Limits."

Briefings

Center

A bird fills up the
streamside bush
with wasteful song,
capsizes waterfall,
mill run, and
superhighway
to
song's improvident
center
lost in the green
bush green
answering bush:
wind varies:
the noon sun casts
mesh refractions
on the stream's amber
bottom
and nothing at all gets,
nothing gets
caught at all.

Mechanics

A clover blossom's a province:
actually: florets cluster helical
villages with visible streets:
down the main arteries a ways
leaffarms produce common sustenance:
the kingbee when all is ready
visits and tries the yellow-doored
purplish houses for virgin
sweet, feeds in winged spells,
rumples everything, and leaves behind
not as a gift or fee—seed, seed.

Up

A clown kite, my
self rustles
up
to any gust:
warps & whucks
the wind: O
my blustering orange
and striped green
immensities!
I get sometimes so
good
tickled at my
self I slip
flat down and
windless
make no
show of grief.

After Yesterday

After yesterday
afternoon's strungled
clouds and white rain
the mockingbird
in the backyard
untied the drops from
leaves and twigs
with a long singing.

Event

A leaf fallen is
fallen
throughout the universe
and
from the instant of
its fall, for
all time gone
and to come:

worlds jiggle in
webs, drub
in leaf lakes,
squiggle in
drops of ditchwater:

size and place
begin, end,
time is allowed
in event's instant:
away or
at home, universe and
leaf try
to fall: occur.

High & Low

A mountain risen
in me
I said
this implacability
must be met:
so I climbed
the peak:
height shook and
wind leaned
I said what
kind of country is
this anyhow and
rubbled
down the slopes to
small rock
and scattered weed.

Peracute Lucidity

A perspicuity like a sanctuary: against
the pond a pavilion, led to by a glide
of stairs, set right and accurately

gauged: the bobolink in the dusk bush
says a closing say-so: *bunk*
bunk the frog maintains and aims his

lofty eyes: just above the brookfall's
shaggy seams and rags, clarity's chapel
bodied by hung-in boughs: and

widening out over the pond, the blown
cathedral luminous with evening glass:
I go out there and sit

till difference and event yield to
perfect composure: then the stars
come out and question every sound, the brook's.

Increment

Applause is a shower
to the watertable of
self regard:
in the downpour
the watertable's irrelevant
but after the shower passes
possibility takes on
an extensive millimeter.

Bees Stopped

Bees stopped on the rock
and rubbed their headparts and wings
rested then flew on:
ants ran over the whitish greenish reddish
plants that grow flat on rocks
and people never see
because nothing should grow on rocks:
I looked out over the lake
and beyond to the hills and trees
and nothing was moving
so I looked closely
along the lakeside
under the old leaves of rushes
and around clumps of drygrass
and life was everywhere
so I went on sometimes whistling

Storm

Branches broken,
the clean meat at the branch knot
turned out white,
traveled by cleared
white light: certain

consequences are
irreversible, arrangements
lost to
death's and black's
scavenging the sweet grain:
well but weakness
went sacrificed to the wind

and the trees, clarified,
compress rootstrength
into remaining flesh
and the leaves that shake
in the aftermath shake
in a safe, tested place.

Two Possibilities

Coming out of the earth and going
into the earth compose
an interval or arc where
what to do's

difficult to fix: if it's
the coming
out that answers, should one with all
thrust come out and

rise to imagination's limit, leaving
earthiness, maximally
to mark the change, much below:
if it's

going in, should one flatten out on
coming, lie low
among bush
and rock, and keep the residence

near the palm of the hand, the
gross engrossed and palpable:
well, there is an interval designed,
apparently, for design.

Medicine for Tight Spots

Consider big-city
tensions
rurally unwound,

high-tension lines that
loft through the countryside,
give off

"wirelings"
and fine-up to houses
cool as a single volt:

there are so many ways to approach the problems:
reproach:
best of all the by-pass and set-aside: the

intelligence has never been called for
because as usually
manifested it's

too formulated to swim
unformulable reality's
fall-out insistences:

just think how woodsy roads
shade spangled
wind up big-city printed circuits:

if the mind becomes what it sees or
makes how it works
I know which way I'm headed:

won't bushes bust us
mild:
won't the streams

ravel us loose:
won't we be untold
by sweetwater tongues.

Brooks & Other Notions

Currents figure
you can see them
they boil out
of themselves &
slice in
from both
sides
a downward crease steady at
the moving burial:

in the wind too
you can feel them
spell
themselves along the
arm, watch them
against an elm
or
multiple on puddles:

below speech
mind
figures motion,
plunges or takes
a turn: grief's

a common
form of going:
its letters rise &
spiel away expressly
inexact.

Cougar

Deprived like the cougar
into heights

I knew huge
air, rock
burn,

lightning, sun,
ice,

gained
insouciance:

bend, bend
the stream called high:
but I climbed higher

knowing what
takes rock away.

This Black Rich Country

Dispossess me of belief:
between life and me obtrude
no symbolic forms:

grant me no mission: let my
mystical talents be beasts
in dark trees: thin the wire

I limp in space, melt it
with quick heat, let me walk
or fall alone: fail

me in all comforts:
hide renown behind the tomb:
withdraw beyond all reach of faith:

leave me this black rich country,
uncertainty, labor, fear: do not
steal the rewards of my mortality.

Attention

Down by the bay I
kept in mind
at once
the tips of all the rushleaves
and so
came to know
balance's cost and true:
somewhere though in the whole field
is the one
tip
I will someday lose out of mind
and fall through.

Return

1

drought continuing
the stems
drop their leaves

healing hard the pulvinal
scars and
dangling buzzards

drop to sleeps
in ledge and
cactus shade, to rockheld

reservoirs of night
and
sidewinder from the

stinging air
holds
his tongue

2

I have come a long way
without arriving
torn songs up

from the roots of weeds
but made no
silence sing:

climbed the peak but
found no foothold
higher than the ground

3

should I roll
rocks
down the slope

to learn
the thunder of
my being:

should I call out,
echolocation fixing me
against a certain wall:

should I break
a switch
and whirling inscribe

a circle round me
to know my
center and periphery

4

the leaves drop:
wolves thinning
like moons run through scuds of sage:

moon cloud shadows
sail gulfs
through a wild terrain

This Bright Day

Earth, earth!
day, this bright day
again—once more
showers of dry spruce gold,
the poppy flopped broad open and delicate
from its pod—once more,
all this again: I've had many
days here with these stones and leaves:
like the sky, I've taken on a color
and am still:
the grief of leaves,
summer worms, huge blackant
queens bulging
from weatherboarding, all that
will pass
away from me that I will pass into,
none of the grief
cuts less now than ever—only I
have learned the
sky, the day sky, the blue
obliteration of radiance:
the night sky,
pregnant, lively,
tumultuous, vast—the grief

again in a higher scale
of leaves and poppies:
space, space—
and a grief of things.

Look for My White Self

Find me diffuse, leached colorless,
gray as an inner image with no clothes
along the shallows of windrows: find

me wasted by hills,
conversion mountain blue in sight
offering its ritual cone of white:

over the plain I came long years,
drawn by gaze: a flat land with
some broken stems, no gullies,

sky matched square inch with
land in staying interchange: found
confusing hills, disconcerting names
and routes, differences locked
in seamless unities:

so look for my white self, age clear,
time cleaned: there is the mountain:
even now my blue

ghost may be
singing on that height of snow.

Undersea

Foraminiferal millennia
bank and spill but
even so
time's under pressure of
diatomaceous event,
divisions a moment
arcs across:
                desperate
for an umbrella, net, longpole,
or fan: so much
to keep for paradigm,
so much to lose.

Auto Mobile

For the bumps bangs & scratches of
collisive encounters
madam
I through time's ruts and weeds
sought you, metallic, your
stainless steel flivver:
I have banged you, bumped
and scratched, side-swiped,
momocked & begommed you &
your little flivver still
works so well.

Wagons

Going west
we finally hit
the sea hills, halted
& went down to
see shells, touch
sand and surf, the
peculiar new conditions,
the anguish perfect
that the sun still
took its gold away:
the waves harmless
unharmable posed
no shapes we could
wrestle to the ground:
turning back like
going down ever
diminishes: we
decided maybe we
would hold but
never turn back
and never go down.

September Drift

Hardly anything flies north these days
(a jay occasionally makes the bleak
decision): the robin, sitting on a high
dead elm limb, looks melancholy with
leisure: he thinks, probably: I wonder
how or of what: small bark-searching

birds drift through the shrubs and trees,
the usual feeding, but in one direction:
I guess I won't go anywhere myself, not
that I don't rustle somewhere deep
and remember ice and wolves: I'll stay
to imagine everything can get back.

Civics

Hard up for better lays (with
fewer diseases)
a less qualified gliding,
he took
amelioration seriously,
thought the poor deserved better
dreams, that
taxes should husband
unwed mothers, house
the losing mad,
raised money for
churches
& otherwise by rising
and increasing
spent himself so his old
eat-up woman got
little of his coin:
there are a number of possibilities.

He Held Radical Light

He held radical light
as music in his skull: music
turned, as
over ridges immanences of evening light
rise, turned
back over the furrows of his brain
into the dark, shuddered,
shot out again
in long swaying swirls of sound:

reality had little weight in his transcendence
so he
had trouble keeping
his feet on the ground, was
terrified by that
and liked himself, and others, mostly
under roofs:
nevertheless, when the
light churned and changed

his head to music, nothing could keep him
off the mountains, his
head back, mouth working,
wrestling to say, to cut loose

from the high, unimaginable hook:
released, hidden from stars, he ate,
burped, said he was like any one
of us: demanded he
was like any one of us.

Locus

Here
it is
the middle of April
(and a day or so more)

and
the small oak
down in
the
hollow is
lit up (winter-burned, ice-gold
leaves on)
at sundown,
ruin transfigured to

stillest shining:
I let it as center
go
and
can't believe
our peripheral
speed.

Circles

I can't decide whether
the backyard stuff's
central or irrelevant:
how matted rank the mint is! and
some of the iris stalks are so
crooked rich
the blossoms can't burst
(scant weeds
pop their flowers fast) loose
and the pansies keep
jointing up another blooming tier:
I can't figure out what
the whole green wish again
is, tips pushing hard into
doing the same, last
year again, the year before:
something nearer than
the pleasure of
circles drives into the next
moment and the next.

Working Still

I can't think of a thing to uphold:
the carborundum plant snows
sift-scum on the slick, outgoing river
and along the avenues car wheels

float in a small powder: my made-up
mind idles like a pyramid: oxides
"under proper atmospheric conditions" become
acids and rain a fine broad bleaching:

man's a plant parasite: so I drop
down to the exchange, $CO_2 \longleftrightarrow O_2$, and
find dread there, just dread: too
much care fuddles me dull:

beef hormones bloom monstrous
with tenderness:
but I won't take up the scaring cause
and can't think of a thing to uphold.

Tooling Up

I cut a new thread on it this morning,
smeared a little dab (a small glob) of
pipedope around (for perfect sealing,
should the opportunity arise or
withdrawal prove premature) and
stuck myself out again: a
formal—possibly too formal—stance,
a willed extension, as if in
expectation of pain:
well but I've done my share: my
mind's at ease: I'm
obviously out, my
intentions are obviously firm.

Father

I dreamed my father flicked
in his grave
then like a fish in water
wrestled with the ground
surfaced and wandered:
I could not find him
through woods, roots, mires
in his bad shape: and
when I found him he was
dead again and had to be
re-entered in the ground:
I said to my mother I still
have you: but out of the
dream I know she died
sixteen years before his
first death:
as I become a child again
a longing that will go away
only with my going grows.

Sumerian

I have grown a marsh dweller
subject to floods and high winds,
drinking brackish water on long hunts,
brushing gnat smoke
from clumps of reeds, have known

the vicissitudes of silt, of
shifting channels flush
by dark upland rains, of mounds
rising no more firmly than
monsters from the water:

on the southern salty
banks near the gulf the ducks
and flying vees of geese have
shunned me: the bouncing spider's net,
strung wet over narrows of reeds, has
broken terror dawn cold across my face:

rising with a handful of broken shells
from sifted underwater mud
I have come to know how high
the platform is, beyond approach,
of serenity and blue temple tiles.

Hippie Hop

I have no program for
saving this world or scuttling
the next: I know no political,
sexual, racial cures: I make
analogies, my bucketful of
flowers: I give flowers to people
of all policies, sexes, and races
including the vicious, the
uncertain, and the white.

Garden

I have sung
delphiniums
seasonless, seedless
out of debris,

stone-white asters
out of shale:
I've made it this far
turning between made sights

and recognitions:
and now
if everything becomes,
as it could,

naturalized, returned,
I may pick hyacinths
here real and tender
in the ruse.

Hymn IV

I hold you responsible for
every womb's neck
clogged with
killing growth

and for ducks on the bay
barking like hounds
all night
their wintering dreams

responsible for every action of
the brain that gives
me mind
and for all light

for the fishroe's
birth spawning forage to
night eels
nosing the tidal banks

I keep you existent at least as
a ghost crab
moon-extinguished his crisp
walk silenced on broken shells

answering at least as
the squiggling copepod
for the birthing and aging of
life's all-clustered grief

You have enriched us with
fear and contrariety
providing the searcher
confusion for his search

teaching by your snickering
wisdom an autonomy
for man
Bear it all

and keep me from my enemies'
wafered concision and zeal
I give you back to yourself
whole and undivided

The Mark

I hope I'm
not right
where frost
strikes the
butterfly
in the back
between
the wings.

Loft

I live in a bodiless loft,
no joists, beams,
or walls:

I huddle high,
arch my back against the stiff
fact of coming down:

my house admits to being
only above the level of most
perception:

I shudder and make do:
I don't look down.

Poetics

I look for the way
things will turn
out spiralling from a center,
the shape
things will take to come forth in

so that the birch tree white
touched black at branches
will stand out
wind-glittering
totally its apparent self:

I look for the forms
things want to come as

from what black wells of possibility,
how a thing will
unfold:

not the shape on paper—though
that, too—but the
uninterfering means on paper:

not so much looking for the shape
as being available
to any shape that may be
summoning itself
through me
from the self not mine but ours.

Working with Tools

I make a simple assertion
like a nice piece of stone
and you
alert to presence and entrance
man your pick and hammer

and by chip and deflection
distract simplicity
and cut my assertion
back to mangles, little heaps:

well, baby, that's the way
you get along: it's all right,
I understand such
ways of being afraid:
sometimes you want my come-on

hard, something to
take in and be around:
sometimes you want
a vaguer touch: I understand
and won't give assertion up.

Doubling the Nerve

In the bleak time look for no cooperation
from the birds: crows show up, black blatant
clarions in the gawky branches, to dominate
the rain's dark: grackles on sprung hinges
grate from tree to tree, around:
                                    remember
the redbird then in the floral plum, the
bluebird nesting in the apple bough:
remember the white streak in the woodpecker's
wings against shadblow:
                                    expect abundance
to yield nothing to privation, no easing
off by contrary song: the quiet world, so
quiet, needs to cut its definitions wide
so snow can rinse across the hard lake.

Making

In wingbar light
the mockingbird
takes the day into
making
takes the clouds still
shipping stars
takes the spring trees'
black small leaves
and with staid motions
and many threads
brings into
view
lightens
and when morning
shows sings
not a whit more beautifully
because it has been dark.

Dominion

I said
Mr. Schafer
did you get up to see the comet:

and
he said
Oh no
let it go by, I don't care:

he has leaves to rake
and the
plunger on his washing machine isn't working right:

he's not amused
by ten-million-mile tails
or any million-mile-an-hour
universal swoosh

or
frozen gases
lit by disturbances

across our
solar arcs

Round

I sat down
from too much
spinning & spun
the big spin's calm:
I said
this is
like it is:

bluebirds
stripped my shoelaces
for nesting:
pill bugs took the cool
under my shoesoles
and weeds, sprung up,
made me their

windbreak:
I said
this is
like it is
and got up turning
out of the still into
the spinning dance.

Tight

I should have had my macadam
driveway re-sealed this fall but
saved a few bucks & let it
go: now the rain pools
out there and the pools
graduate toward each other
with long necks of lonesome
longing: but there's a sort
of idle rain, like today's,
when the drops, large &

sparse, pop huge bubbles
that cruise around smooth
uneventful country: I sat out
there watching a couple of
hours from the garage and got
rapturous trying to think why
that particular show (not to
mention how) ever got devised:
it makes me wonder which way
the economy should be sent.

The Woodsroad

I stop on
the woodsroad,
listen:
I take myself in:

I let go the locust's
burr-squall, pointless,
high in the pine:
I turn all

the clouds crossing
above me loose:
I drop free of
the fern's sori:

I zoom home through,
as if hailstruck,
caterpillar-pocked
whiteoak leaves:

I take myself
all in, let go &
float free: then
break into

clouds, white dots on
dead stalks, robin
mites: then, I'm here:
I listen: call.

WCW

I turned in
by the bayshore
and parked,
the crosswind
hitting me hard
side the head,
the bay scrappy
and working:
what a
way to read
Williams! till
a woman came
and turned
her red dog loose
to sniff
(and piss
on)
the dead horseshoe
crabs.

Saying

I went out on
a rustling day
and
lectured the willow:
it nodded profoundly
and held
out many arms:
I held my
arms up and said things:
I spoke up:
I turned into and
from the wind:
I looked all around:
dusk, sunless,
starless, came:
the wind
fell and left us
in the open
still and bent.

Looking Over the Acreage

I wonder what I should do now:
probably
I should wait
for the onset or oncoming of a large order,
an aqueduct perhaps
with an endless (theoretically) echo of arches
but which a valley would
break into individual aqueductal shape:
or perhaps an abecedarian procedure
though there are some
problems there
(not everyone is agreed on
what is what)
or I could riffle through the zodiac:
then there are
triads, pentads, dodecahedra,
earth-water-air-fire,
the loft
from indivisibility to all-is-one
(which is where nothing is anything):
descents are less usual
having associations of undesirability
(cities, societies are
exclusive):

the great advantage of an overall arbitrary
order is that one
need not wait until he has earned an order
but may go ahead with some serenity arch
by arch
content if minor forms appear:
one may do that:
I don't know what to do:
no matter what I think I'm probably going to wind up
in both wings of another balance:
  fabulous, ex
  cit
  ing, over
  populated
  Hong Kong: yeah.

Gain

Last night my mind limped
down the halls of its citadel,
wavered by the lofty columns
as if a loosened door had
let the wind try inside
for what could go:
dreamed of the fine pane-work
of lofty windows it
would not climb to again to see,
of curved attics aflight with
angels it would not
disturb again: felt the
tenancy of its own house,
shuffled to the great door and
looked out into its permanent dwelling.

Off

Morning's the woman time of day,
light rising
as in a small failure,
the parting of fog
to cloud,
the casual centerless thunder
and the rain beginning
so sporadic
the eye can hardly weave the evidence
and then rain
full rain
windless,
the iris unshook from its beads,
the firs like old old
men dripping their bottoms wet:
I catch my breath
I throw my clothes on
I have to get out of the house
and, out, my eyes'
concision shoots to kill.

Treaties

My great wars close:
ahead, papers,
signatures, the glimmering
in shade of
leaf and raised wine:
orchards, orchards,
vineyards, fields:
spiralling slow time while
the medlar
smarts and glows and
empty nests
come out in the open:
fall rain then stirs
the black creek and
the small leaf slips in.

Convergence

My sorrows he said
begin so
deep they join only
at extreme, skinny height:
so he climbed

and water fell
smooth, chasms
lifted into ripples
and earth's slow
curve

merged, emerged:
he stood capable
poised
on the peak of
illusion's pyramid.

Project

My subject's
still the wind still
difficult to
present
being invisible:
nevertheless should I
presume it not
I'd be compelled
to say
how the honeysuckle bushlimbs
wave themselves:
difficult
beyond presumption

North Jersey

Ninth-circle concrete
bending in
high suasions like
formal reductions of
perfect fears: refineries
oiling the air:
burnt reeds, a chemical
scald: gouged land &
shoved mounds:
and man
burning fast motions along
the steely wreaths,
the steely wreaths.

Ship

Nobody comes here to stay: that's
incredible: and nothing to stay:
the bird tilts tail-up in the high
branch and tilts time away:
well, I don't want to think about that:
the phony comfort about timelessness
time is supposed to work back
into: I've seen no sign of that:
nothing on the re-make or comeback: the
crest breaks, whatever side the sea's on:
the crest bears in and out in a single
motion, not a single point unmoving:
men and women in your loveliness, I cry
nothing against the wall forever giving in.

Play

Nothing's going to become of anyone
except death:
        therefore: it's okay
to yearn
too high:
the grave accommodates
swell rambunctiousness &
ruin's not
compromised by magnificence:

that cut-off point
liberates us to the
common disaster: so
        pick a perch—
apple branch for example in bloom—
tune up
and

drill imagination right through necessity:
it's all right:
it's been taken care of:

is allowed, considering

Spinejacking

One of these days I'm gonna leave you, baby:
I know it: I can tell:
my bellyfat shakes and knows:
one of these days I'm gonna just
up and outsy: like that:
my dog knows: he
turns around a lot lately:
I don't know if the parrot knows:
it isn't just lately she started scratching:
you always were a kind of bushy bitch:
one of these days I'm gonna just pack off:
you get to make some new
arrangements, then: you like to change
things around, change this one:
one of these days I'm gonna leave you, baby:
I know it: I can tell:
my bellyfat shakes and knows.

Shore Fog

On the cedars and yews
this morning
big drops
(as of rain)
held by finny hands
(but not rain):
fog kept the night all
night awake
and left this morning
in addition to these
big clarities
a close-worked white drift
too multiple to
prevent some dozing.

Meteorology

Reality's gossed guzzlings,
bristle-eyed
in light
mare's-tails of bleached
speech have
unmaimed the handshrunk
blessings,
declotted the conveyances:
the bleakies
sung against
sweep soaring (that's
delightful) into
high seed
but come back
heebies and harpies
ever
scratching &
fartching:
confine self to
"extremities & superfices"
the unenterable core's rusty
lode shut up.

Exotic

Science outstrips
other modes &
reveals more of
the crux of the matter
than we can calmly
handle

Hosts

Secrets are slimber black worms
whose appetites are red:
they ball up with searching periphery:
sometimes they string out, roam
the body in a panic of mismanagement:
it's nice when they slacken
(wads of worthy long fellows) and go
to sleep: often they're
sleepless:
some people have more
than others which
makes a difference.

Crevice

Seeing into myth is
knowledge myth can't sanctify:
separating symbol and
translucence
disembodies belief:
still, nothing's changed:
the slope that
falls here toward the lake
has held
since the first mind figured
in and out of shape:
but a constant in change
no hand or sight has
given definition to:
how are we new from the slow
alterations now:
we stand around dazed
and separate, sunless and eventful:
mind can't charge the slope:
again we've fallen wise.

Transducer

Solar floes
big as continents
plunge rasping
against each other:
the noise
flaring into space,
into thinner & thinner
material means
becomes two million
degrees of heat.

Mean

Some drippage and spillage in
active situations:
efficiency's detritus,
fall-out from happenstance:
a, probably calculable,
instrank of frabigity:
people accustomed to the wide terrain
know, with little alarm, some
clumps are dissolving:
singular's the terrible view
from which the classy gods
take up glassy lives.

Banking

Sometimes I see an
enormous loveliness:
I say help like a
deprived nation:
this loveliness
moves & the motion
starves rivers:
the air where
this motion
moves feels
expensive: I go
out where this
is going by and
come back in narrow
about the nose
with some
wilted plants & all
my old peeled sticks.

Elegy for a Jet Pilot

The blast skims
over the string
of takeoff lights
and
relinquishing
place and time
lofts to
separation:
the plume, rose
silver, grows
across the
high-lit evening
sky: by this
Mays Landing creek
shot pinecones,
skinned huckleberry
bush, laurel
swaths define
an unbelievably
particular stop.

Countering

The crystal of reason
grows
down
into my loves and
terrors, halts
or muddles
flow,
casting me to
shine or break:

the savage peoples
wood slopes, shore rocks
with figures of dream
who struggle
to save or
have his life:

to keep the
life and
shape, to keep
the sphere, I hide
contours,
progressions between

turning lines,
toward the higher
reason
that contains the war
of shape and loss
at rest.

The Quince Bush

The flowering quince bush
on the back hedge has been
run through by a morning
glory vine

and this morning three blooms
are open as if for all light,
sound, and motion: their adjustment
to light is

pink, though they reach for
stellar reds and core violets:
they listen as if for racket's
inner silence

and focus, as if to starve, all motion:
patterns of escaped sea
they tip the defeated, hostile,
oceanic wind:

elsewhere young men scratch and fire:
a troubled child shudders to a freeze:
an old man bursts finally and
rattles down

clacking slats: the caterpillar pierced
by a wasp egg blooms inside with
the tender worm: wailing
walls float

luminous with the charge of grief:
a day pours through a morning glory
dayblossom's adequate, poised,
available center.

Square

The formulation that
saves damns:
consequently (unsavable)
a periphery riffler
I thread the
outskirts of mandate,
near enough
to be knowingly away &
far enough away to
wind and snap through
riddling underbrush.

Autumn Song

The large is gone—well, it
was mostly vacant: the big
time,
a past and future scoop,
gone, too,
but it was too
big to move much:
I picked up a wet leaf
today: it
left its shape moist
on the macadam
and there was an earthworm
his arteries
shining in the brilliant light—
it really was brilliant today—and
he
panicked at both ends
with the threat of drying out:
a basic
concern I shared with him
and share with him
for I lifted him with the leaf
and took him to the grass:
I'll bet he knows now

he can be seen through and turn
into a little thong:
I knew it all along though I'm
not in grass
and the leaves that fall
give me no sense of refuge.

Early Morning
in Early April

The mist rain this morning made glass,
a glittery preponderance, hung baubles
spangled to birch-twig jewelry,

and made the lawn support, item by
item, the air's weight, a lesson as a
various instruction with a theme: and

how odd, the maple branches underlaced
with glaring beadwork: what to make of it:
what to make of a mist whose characteristic

is a fine manyness coming dull in a wide
oneness: what to make of the glass
erasures, glass: the yew's partly lost.

Reversal

The mt in my head surpasses you
I said

becomes at the base
more nearly incalculable with

bush
more divisive with suckers and roots

and at the peak
far less visible

plumed and misty
opening from unfinal rock to air:

arrogance arrogance
the mt said

the wind in your days
accounts for this arrogance

The Confirmers

The saints are gathering at the real
places, trying tough skin on sharp
    conscience,
endurance in the hot spots—
searching out to define, come up
against, mouth
the bitterest bit:
you can hear them yelping
down in the dark greeny groves of
    condemnation:
their lips slice back
with jittery suctions, cold
insweeps of conjured grief:
if they, footloose, wham up the
precise damnation,
    consolation
may be no more than us trudging
down from paunchy dinners,
swatting hallelujah arms at
dusk bugs and telling them pure
terror has obviously made them
earnest of mind and of motion lithe.

Involved

They say last night radiation
storms spilled down the meridians,
cool green tongues of solar
flares, non-human & not
to be humanized, licking at
human life: an arctic
air mass shielded us: had I been
out I'd have said,
knowing them masked, burn me: or
thanks for the show:
my spine would have flared
sympathetic colors:
as it is I slept through,
burning from a distant source.

Admission

The wind high along the headland,
mosquitoes keep low: it's
good to be out:
schools of occurring whitecaps
come into the bay,
leap, and dive:
gulls stroll
long strides down the shore wind:
every tree shudders utterance:
motions—sun, water, wind, light—
intersect, merge: here possibly
from the crest of the right moment
one might break away from the final room.

Mission

The wind went over
me
saying
why are you so distressed:

oh I said I
can't seem to make
anything
round enough to last:

but why
the wind
said
should you be so distressed

as if anything here belonged to you
as if anything here were your concern.

Cut the Grass

The wonderful workings of the world: wonderful,
wonderful: I'm surprised half the time:
ground up fine, I puff if a pebble stirs:

I'm nervous: my morality's intricate: if
a squash blossom dies, I feel withered as a stained
zucchini and blame my nature: and

when grassblades flop to the little red-ant
queens burring around trying to get aloft, I blame
my not keeping the grass short, stubble

firm: well, I learn a lot of useless stuff, meant
to be ignored: like when the sun sinking in the
west glares a plane invisible, I think how much

revelation concealment necessitates: and then I
think of the ocean, multiple to a blinding
oneness and realize that only total expression

expresses hiding: I'll have to say everything
to take on the roundness and withdrawal of the deep dark:
less than total is a bucketful of radiant toys.

The Limit

This left hand
side is
the clear edge of
imposition: the other the
thrusting and breaking to possibility:
in between
a tumbling, folding under,
amounting to downward
progression:
the prisoner is not much enamored of compression:
I wonder if this slight
tumbling, brookish, is a large enough motion
to prevent lodged sticks & harrow beavers:
apparently it
can
reach out broadly across the page in space-hungry gesture:
the events a stick makes
coming down a
brook
scraping the bottom
of the ledge-smooth spill—such
events exist in memory
& possibility as in
a silver radiance: the salience,

in a bodiless arrogance,
must preserve
algal tracings or it
loses further (already scared of loss)
ground for possible self-imaginings:
interwork, interwork, it's interwork
that pays with mind because mind
(if an entelechy)—
      shifting over here
      will suggest a tone-gap, slant,
      a redshift as of direction

Concerning the Exclusions
of the Object

Today I
looked for myself,

head full of
stars,

cosmic
dust in my teeth,

and small,
lost

as earth in such a
world, I

fell around my
cell's space

and said
I must be here—how

can I get the seeker
home into these jaws:

how
can I expel these roomy stars?

The Makers

We slung do out of the rosy alligator
and
finding him somewhat flattened
    opened

our kits to engines of more
precise destruction
and set in to settled, intense abuse:

lovers and haters of dragons found
themselves
grievously ready to do a little slicing

back:

it was hilarious, stupendous, and quite painful
until
ritualization so overtook us all

that the only product dropping out from
    slitting & stitching was
pocketbooks pocketbooks pocketbooks
from the colorful land of the

Levitation

What are you doing
up there
said the ground
that disastrous to seers
and saints
is always around
evening scores, calling down:

I turned
cramped in abstraction's gilded loft
and
tried to think of something beautiful to say:

why
I said failing
I'm investigating the
coming together of things:

the ground
tolerant of such
widened without sound

while I turning
harmed my spine against
the peak's inner visionless ribs—

heels free
neck locked in the upward drift—

and even the ground I think
grew shaky
thinking something might be up there
able to get away.

Medium

What small grace comes must
count hard

and then
belong to the poem that is in need

not to my own redemption
except
as the mirror gives back the dream:

since I am guilty
any crime
will do
to pour my costly anguish to:
but

payment is exact,
strict and clear: the purchase
never comes

or if so becomes a song
that takes its blessings to itself
and gets away.

Transfer

When the bee lands the
morning glory bloom
dips some and weaves:
    the coming true of
    weight
    from weightless wing-held
    air
    seems at the touch
    implausible.

Monday

Windowjarring gusts again
this morning:
the surf slapped back white:
shore cherry bushes
trying to
stay put or get away:
the vague storm's
aroused a weekend of
hypochondria: today
the doctors' offices
froth with all
that tried to stay unruffled.

Pluralist

Winds light & variable break
upward out
of cones or drop cones down
that turn up
umbrellalike from the
ground

and even the maple tree's large
enough to express contrary
notions
one side going west & the
other east or northeast or one
up & the other
down: multiple angling:

the nodding, twisting, the
stepping out & back
is like being of two minds
at least
and with the comforting
(though scary) exemplum
that maple trees
go nowhere at all

Here & Now

Yes but
it's October and the leaves
are going
fast: rain weighted
them and then
a breeze
sent them in shoals clear across
the street

revealing
especially in the backyard
young maple
branch-tip buds that assume
time as far away as
the other side of the sun

The Run-Through

You're sick:
you're on your back:
it's hot:
they take off a leg:
you wake up and feel,
both hands:
you develop pride
in the sewmanship
and show it:

a tube in your skull bursts:
you bleed half
still:
with one arm
you show how
the other flops:
you show, show:
speechless with pantomime:

you're on your back:
it's hot:
they take the other one off:
then you fail
some

with the difficulty
of redundancy:

you're on your back:
you are heavy and hard:
your heart bursts and you are weightless:
you ride to a high stillness:
in death's cure, you exit right.

The Put-Down Come On

You would think I'd be a specialist in contemporary
literature: novels, short stories, books of poetry,
my friends write many of them: I don't read much
and some drinks are too strong for me: my empty-headed

contemplation is still where the ideas of permanence
and transience fuse in a single body, ice, for example,
or a leaf: green pushes white up the slope: a maple
leaf gets the wobbles in a light wind and comes loose

half-ready: where what has always happened and what
has never happened before seem for an instant reconciled:
that takes up most of my time and keeps me uninformed:
but the slope, after maybe a thousand years, may spill

and the ice have a very different look withdrawing into
the lofts of cold: only a little of that kind of
thinking flashes through: but turning the permanent also
into the transient takes up all the time that's left.

The City Limits

When you consider the radiance, that it does not withhold
itself but pours its abundance without selection into every
nook and cranny not overhung or hidden; when you consider

that birds' bones make no awful noise against the light but
lie low in the light as in a high testimony; when you consider
the radiance, that it will look into the guiltiest

swervings of the weaving heart and bear itself upon them,
not flinching into disguise or darkening; when you consider
the abundance of such resource as illuminates the glow-blue

bodies and gold-skeined wings of flies swarming the dumped
guts of a natural slaughter or the coil of shit and in no
way winces from its storms of generosity; when you consider

that air or vacuum, snow or shale, squid or wolf, rose or lichen,
each is accepted into as much light as it will take, then
the heart moves roomier, the man stands and looks about, the

leaf does not increase itself above the grass, and the dark
work of the deepest cells is of a tune with May bushes
and fear lit by the breadth of such calmly turns to praise.